ISBN 978-1-330-98928-9
PIBN 10130433

English
Français
Deutsche
Italiano
Español
Português

www.forgottenbooks.com

Mythology Photography **Fiction**
Fishing Christianity **Art** Cooking
Essays Buddhism Freemasonry
Medicine **Biology** Music **Ancient
Egypt** Evolution Carpentry Physics
Dance Geology **Mathematics** Fitness
Shakespeare **Folklore** Yoga Marketing
Confidence Immortality Biographies
Poetry **Psychology** Witchcraft
Electronics Chemistry History **Law**
Accounting **Philosophy** Anthropology
Alchemy Drama Quantum Mechanics
Atheism Sexual Health **Ancient History**
Entrepreneurship Languages Sport
Paleontology Needlework Islam
Metaphysics Investment Archaeology
Parenting Statistics Criminology
Motivational

GERALD MASSEY: POE PROPHET AND MYSTI

BY B. O. FLOWER, WITH
ILLUSTRATIONS BY
LAURA LEE.

THE ARENA PUBLISHING
CO., BOSTON, MASS.
MDCCCXCV.

This book is inscribed to my wife,
HATTIE C. FLOWER,
whose noble life, and fine, inspiring thought, have been a
constant aid in all I have
endeavored to accom-
plish for freedom,
justice and truth.

THIS little work briefly discusses the life and work of one of England's poets of the people, who deserves far more from the hands of those who love justice, freedom and truth than he has received. I have purposely quoted very freely from the writings of Mr. Massey, because I am persuaded that, in order to know the true self or the spiritual ego of an individual, we must see his soul in action, see him battling with injustice or error, when the profound depths of his being are stirred by some high and saving truth; for then is revealed the spirit, unconscious for the moment of the fetters of environment or the trammels of artificiality which surround us all.   Then, the curtain is raised and we catch a glimpse of the holiest of holies of the human soul. This revelation of the higher self is very marked in the noblest lines of a true poet. I have had a further purpose in view in thus introducing the poet through his own words. I desired to bring the high, fine thought of Gerald Massey to the attention of men and women of conviction, believing that his noble ideals, his passionate appeals for justice, his prophetic glimpse of the coming day, would serve to awaken some sleeping souls, while they would strengthen others in their purpose to consecrate life's best endeavors to the cause of earth's miserables and to the diffusion of light.

In the third chapter I have indicated some striking points of resemblance between the writings of Massey and Whittier. The former is passionately in love with the beauty in common life. He is a tireless reformer, hating injustice more than he loves life, and he possesses a spiritual insight equalled by few modern poets. These also are marked characteristics of our New England Quaker poet. The titles poet, prophet and seer are as applicable to the one as to the other, although Mr. Massey possesses less intuitional perception than Whittier. What he lacks here, however, is balanced by his passion for truth, which has led him to search profoundly for hints and facts that demonstrate the reality of another life.

Mr. Massey has been too fearless and too persistent a reformer to be appreciated in his time, but his words and worth will be treasured in the brighter day, when we shall see dawning a social order which shall end enforced " slavery for man, prostitution for woman, and ignorance for the child."

As a poet of the common life who has revealed new beauties within and without the homes of the humble, I admire him;

as a fearless truth-seeker who has dared to incur the scoffs and sneers of conventionalism and the savage hate of ignorance, bigotry and fanaticism, in the cause of truth, I honor him; and because he has been a true prophet of freedom, fraternity and justice, ever loyal to the interest of the oppressed, I love him. Mr. Massey's face has been steadfastly set toward the morning; his thoughts are luminous with the light of the coming age; hence it is not surprising that he has disturbed the bats and owls, or enraged the serpents and tigers in society, who instinctively shrink from the holy candor of truth or the sweet reasonableness of justice.

B. O. FLOWER.

BOSTON, January, 1895.

"She grew a sweet and sinless child."

THERE are in our midst many poets who attract small attention from conventional critics, as they have studiously avoided the praise of conservatism, choosing the byways of duty in preference to the highway of popularity, and always living up to their highest conviction of right. The poor, the oppressed, and the sorrowing have been their special charge. Their lives have been characterized by simplicity, and their words and deeds have inspired unnumbered struggling souls with lofty ideals and nobler conceptions of life. While the wreath of fame has been placed by conservatism on the brows of many whose empty rhymes have conformed to the *dilettante* standard of "art for art's sake," these poets have quietly sung courage, hope and love into the hearts of the people, luring them unconsciously to higher altitudes of spirituality. They have at all times proclaimed the noble altruism of living for others — the song of the to-morrow of civilization. Amid the ambitions and jealousies of life, the strife for fame and gold, they are not found; but where tyranny mocks freedom and the poor cry for justice, their words ring clear and strong. They are the people's saviours, for they help the multitudes into the light of truth and up the path of noble endeavor.

Among this *coterie* of chosen sons of God, whose unpurchasable love of justice and holy candor of soul have rendered it impossible for them to yield to the siren voices of conventionalism, no name is entitled to a more honored place than that of Gerald Massey — the poet-prophet of our day, who has stood for truth and right, while less royal souls have sold their heaven-given birthright for earth's pottage. Had Mr. Massey chosen to devote his rare talent to the humors and dictates of conventionalism, instead of offending the *dilettante* by boldly pleading the cause of the oppressed; had he devoted his gifts to the creation of popular lyrics, instead of compelling his readers to think upon the wrongs of those who suffer through man's inhumanity to man, he would not have remained comparatively obscure and been compelled to eat the bread of poverty. For few men of our century have received higher praise from leading literary critics than this poet of the people. And had wealth been able to flatter him into a fawning sycophant he would have become the idol of a gay, frivolous and amusement-loving class who imagine they are cultured.

But Gerald Massey was a man before he was a poet. His love for justice was greater than his desire for the eider down of luxury or the chaplet of fame. He was the son of a poor man. He himself had tasted the bitterness of want. He possessed the courage of an Elijah and the spirit of an Isaiah. He preferred to reflect the best in his soul and devote his divine gift to the service of justice, rather than conform to the vicious standards which conventionalism demands as the price of popularity and preferment. He championed the cause of the weak, the poor and those whose lives are made bitter by having to bear heavier burdens than rightfully belong to them.

Now, because of this magnificient loyalty to justice and human rights, because he dared to assail the injustice of entrenched plutocracy and the hypocrisy of creedal religion, he has been denied the justice due to his fine poetic talent and his superb manhood. But though ignored, in the main, by conservatism, he has won the hearts of millions who love, suffer and wait. And I believe the future will place him high in the pantheon of England's poets, because he has voiced the real spirit of the on-coming civilization in a truer and braver way than many contemporaries who are basking in popular favor. The following extracts from his writings reflect the dream ever present in the poet's mind. They may be said to contain the keynote of his creed: —

" The first duty of men who have to die is to learn how to live, so as to leave the world, or something in it, a little better than they found it. Our future life must be the natural outcome of this : the root of the whole matter is in *this* life."

We hear the cry for bread with plenty smiling all
    around;
Hill and valley in their bounty blush for man with
    fruitage crowned,

What a merry world it might be, opulent for all
    and aye,
With its lands that ask for labor, and its wealth
    that wastes away!
This world is full of beauty, as other worlds
    above;
And, if we did our duty, it might be full of love.

The leaf-tongues of the forest, and the flower-lips
    of the sod,
The happy birds that hymn their raptures in the
    ear of God,
The summer wind that bringeth music over land
    and sea,
Have each a voice that singeth this sweet song
    of songs to me —
"This world is full of beauty, as other worlds
    above;
And, if we did our duty, it might be full of love."

If faith, and hope, and kindness passed, as coin,
    'twixt heart and heart,
Up through the eye's tear-blindness, how the sudden
    soul should start!

The dreary, dim and desolate should wear a sunny
    bloom,
And love should spring from buried hate, like
    flowers from winter's tomb.
This world is full of beauty, as other worlds
    above;
And, if we did our duty, it might be full of love.

Were truth our uttered language, spirits might talk
    with men,
And God-illumined earth should see the Golden
    Age again;
The burthened heart should soar in mirth like
    morn's young prophet-lark,
And misery's last tear wept on earth quench hell's
    last cunning spark!
This world is full of beauty, as other worlds
    above;
And, if we did our duty, it might be full of love.

Gerald Massey was born in Hertfordshire,
England, in 1828. His father was ex-
tremely poor, and Gerald was compelled at
an early age to enter a factory, and thus

help support a family which knew all the bitterness of biting poverty. Many years of his early life were spent in straw plaiting. At eight he was working twelve hours a day in a silk manufactory, and receiving from nine pence to one shilling and sixpence a week. Very pathetic is the poet's description of the bitter struggle with poverty which marked his early boyhood. Still, without this experience it is doubtful if the world would have been enriched by his clarion cries for justice or the inspiring songs of hope and courage which will be sung and resung until the wealth producer is emancipated and civilization learns her supreme lesson — that Humanity is one.

John Ruskin, who has ever seemed to take a special interest in Gerald Massey, on one occasion wrote the poet — " Your education was a terrible one, but mine was far worse ; " the one having suffered the bitterness of poverty, the other having been the pampered child of wealth. Very few books came into the possession of the poor poet boy, and his time was so taken up that he had few moments for the luxury of reading. He received no instruction save that obtained in a penny school, but his passionate longing for knowledge led him to many fountains of truth which duller minds would never have discerned. The book of nature attracted his eye, her smile wooed him, her voice charmed his ear; his mind unconsciously drank deeply of her truths. Like many another poor boy, Mr. Massey learned the value of knowledge. His mind became a storehouse for truth, rather than a sieve, and his passion for the acquisition of facts, which was awakened before necessity compelled him to enter the rank of the child slaves of factory life, grew stronger as he advanced in years. At a later period he became a deep student along several lines of thought. An overmastering determination to possess the truth and an unflinching loyalty to what he conceived to be right, have been marked characteristics of the poet's life. In him we have a curious combination. He is one of the most graceful and charming lyric poets England has given the world. He is also a seer and philosopher, a mystic and scientific student, a prophet and reformer, while all his work reflects simplicity and purity of life inspired by his high ethical code and lofty faith. For years he has experienced remarkable psychic phenomena within his own home circle. To him have been given test and evidences which have convinced him beyond all peradventure of doubt that his loved ones who have passed from view are neither in the ground nor in some far-off Heavenly City of the Christian, nor yet in the state of Devachan of the Buddhist, but are around about him, in his daily life.

He has had proof palpable and of such a reason-compelling character as to leave no doubt in his mind that his dear ones live, love and move onward. On this point Mr. Massey thus clearly and forcibly expresses his convictions:—

"My faith in our future life is founded upon facts in nature, and realities of my own personal experience; not upon any falsification of natural fact. These facts have been more or less known to me personally during forty years of familiar face-to-face acquaintanceship, therefore my certitude is not premature; they have given me the proof palpable that our very own human identity and intelligence do persist after the blind of darkness has been drawn down in death. He who has plumbed the void of death as I have, and touched this solid ground of fact, has established a faith that can never be undermined nor over-thrown. He has done with the poetry of desolation and despair, the sighs of unavailing regret, and all the passionate wailing of unfruitful pain. *He cannot be bereaved in soul!* And I have had ample testimony that my poems have done welcome work, if only in helping to destroy the tyranny of death, which has made so many mental slaves afraid to live.

"The false faiths are fading; but it is in the light of a truer knowledge. The half Gods are going in order that the whole Gods may come. There is finer fish in the unfathomed sea of the future than any we have yet landed. It is only in our time that the data have been collected for rightly interpreting the past of man, and for portraying the long and vast procession of his slow but never-ceasing progress through the sandy wilderness of an uncultivated earth into the world of work, with the ever-quickening consciousness of a higher, worthier life to come. And without this measure of the human past, we could have no true gauge of the growth that is possible in the future!

"Indeed it seems to me that we are only just beginning to lay hold of this life in earnest: only just standing on the very threshold of true thought; only just now attaining a right mental method of thinking, through a knowledge of evolution; only just getting in line with natural law, and seeking earnestly to stand level-footed on that ground of reality which must ever and everywhere be the one lasting foundation of all that is permanently true."

On the vital social problems which intimately affect the progress of the race, Mr. Massey evinces the clear perceptions of a broad-visioned philosopher. He observes : —

"It is only of late that the tree of knowledge has begun to lose its evil character, to be planted anew, and spread its roots in the fresh ground of every board-school, with its fruits no longer accursed, but made free to all.

We are beginning to see that the worst of the evils now afflicting the human race are man made, and do not come into the world by decree of fate or fiat of God; and that which is man made is also remediable by man. Not by man alone! For woman is about to take her place by his side as true helpmate and ally in carrying on the work of the world, so that we may look upon the fall of man as being gradually superseded by the ascent of woman. And here let me say, parenthetically, that I consider it to be the first necessity for women to obtain the parliamentry franchise before they can hope to stand upon a business footing of practical equality with men; and therefore I have no sympathy with these would-be abortionists, who have been somewhat too " previously " trying to take the life of woman suffrage in embryo before it should have the chance of being brought to birth."

With the keen penetration of a highly intuitive mind, Mr. Massey long ago perceived that wisdom as well as justice demands that woman be accorded a far more exalted place than she has been permitted to occupy in the past, and he has been an untiring advocate of absolute justice and the same wholesome freedom for her as is good for man. I know of no writer of any age who has taken higher grounds for true morality, both within and without the marriage relation, than Mr. Massey. He is one of the few men of our time who have evinced superb courage in demanding that women be protected from involuntary prostitution within the marriage relation. On this important theme he observes : —

"The truth is, that woman at her best and noblest must be monarch of the marriage-bed. We must begin in the creatory if we are to benefit the race, and the woman has got to rescue and take possession of herself, and consciously assume all the responsibilities of maternity, on behalf of the children. No woman has any right to part with the absolute ownership of her own body, but she has the right to be protected against all forms of brute force. No woman has any business to marry anything that is less than a man. No woman has any right to marry any man who will sow the seeds of hereditary disease in her darlings. Not for all the money in the world! No woman has any right, according to the highest law, to bear a child to a man she does not love."

Our poet's high ideal of woman and her true position is beautifully expressed in the following lines : —

My fellow-men, as yet we have but seen
Wife, sister, mother, and daughter — not the queen
Upon her throne, with all her jewels crowned!

Unknowing how to seek, we have not found
Our goddess, waiting her Pygmalion
To woo her into woman from the stone!

Our husbandry hath lacked essential power
To fructify the promise of the flower;
We have not known her nature ripe all round.

We have but seen her beauty on one side
That leaned in love to us with blush of bride:
The pure white lily of all womanhood,
With heart all golden, still is in the bud.

We have but glimpsed a moment in her face
The glory she will give the future race;
The strong, heroic spirit knit beyond
All induration of the diamond.

She is the natural bringer from above,
The earthly mirror of immortal love;

The chosen mouthpiece for the mystic word
Of life divine to speak through, and be heard
With human voice, that makes its heavenward call
Not in one virgin motherhood, but all.

Unworthy of the gift, how have men trod
Her pearls of pureness, swine-like, in the sod!
How often have they offered her the dust
And ashes of the fanned-out fires of lust,
Or, devilishly inflamed with the divine,
Waxed drunken with the sacramental wine!

How have men captured her with savage grips,
To stamp the kiss of conquest on her lips;
As feather in their crest have worn her grace,
Or brush of fox that crowns the hunter's chase;
Wooed her with passions that but wed to fire
With Hymen's torch their own funereal pyre;
Stripped her as slave and temptress of desire;
Embraced the body when her soul was far
Beyond possession as the loftiest star!

Her whiteness hath been tarnished by their touch;
Her promise hath been broken in their clutch;
The woman hath reflected man too much,
And made the bread of life with earthiest leaven.

Our coming queen must be the bride of heaven —
The wife who will not wear her bonds with pride
As adult doll with fripperies glorified;
The mother fashioned on a nobler plan
Than woman who was merely made *from* man.

On the proper rearing of children he has words to say which should appeal to every loving parent:—

"The life we live with them every day is the teaching that tells, and not the precepts uttered weekly that are continually belied by our own daily practices. Give the children a knowledge of natural law, especially in that domain of physical nature which has hitherto been tabooed. If we break a natural law we suffer pain in consequence, no matter whether we know the law or not. This result is not an accident, because it always happens, and is obviously intended to happen. Punishments are not to be avoided by ignorance of effects; they can only be warded off by a knowledge of causes. Therefore nothing but knowledge can help them. Teach the children to become the soldiers of duty instead of the slaves of selfish desire. Show them how the sins against self reappear in the lives of others. Teach them to think of those others as the means of getting out of self. Teach them how the laws of nature work by heredity. . . Children have ears like the very spies of nature herself; eyes that penetrate all subterfuge and pretence. . . Let them be well grounded in the doctrine of development, without which we cannot begin to think coherently. Give them the best material, the soundest method; let the spirit world have a chance as a living influence on them, and then let them do the rest. Never forget that the faculty for seeing is worth all that is to be seen. It is good to set before them the loftiest ideals—not those that are mythical and non-natural, but those that have been lived in human reality. The best ideal of all has to be portrayed by the parents in the realities of life at home. The teaching that goes deepest will be indirect, and the truth will tell most on them when it is overheard. When you are not watching, and the children *are*—that is when the lessons are learned for life."

These are twentieth-century thoughts, and they are pregnant with the truth which will yet make the world glad. One thing which impresses the reader, in all Mr. Massey's works, is his sincerity and his abhorrence of hypocrisy or shams of any kind. This thought, which is present in all his writings, is emphasized in the following passage from his "Devil of Darkness" : —

" The devil and hell of my creed consist in that natural Nemesis which follows on broken laws, and dogs the law breaker, in spite of any belief of his that his sins and their inevitable results can be so cheaply sponged out, as he has been misled to think, through the shedding of innocent blood. Nature knows nothing of the forgiveness for sin. She has no rewards or punishments—nothing but causes and consequences. For example, if you should contract a certain disease and pass it on to your children and their children, all the alleged forgiveness of God will be of no avail if you cannot forgive yourself. Ours is the devil of heredity, working in two worlds at once. Ours is a far more terrible way of realizing the hereafter, when it is brought home to us in concrete fact, whether in this life or the life to come, than any abstract idea of hell or devil can afford. We have to face the facts beforehand—no use to whine over them impotently afterwards, when it is too late. For example :—

In the olden days when immortals
  To earth came visibly down,
There went a youth with an angel
  Through the gate of an Eastern town.
They passed a dog by the roadside,
  Where dead and rotting it lay,
And the youth, at the ghastly odor,
  Sickened and turned away.
He gathered his robes around him,
  And hastily hurried thence ;
But nought annoyed the angel's
  Clear, pure, immortal sense.

By came a lady, lip-luscious,
  On delicate, mincing feet ;
All the place grew glad with her presence,
  All the air about her sweet,
For she came in fragrance floating,
  And her voice most silvery rang ;
And the youth, to embrace her beauty,
  With all his being sprang.
A sweet, delightsome lady :
  And yet, the legend saith,
The angel, while he passed her,
  Shuddered and held his breath !

"Only think of a fine lady who, in this life, had been wooed and flattered, sumptuously clad and delicately fed; for whom the pure, sweet air of heaven had to be perfumed as incense, and the red rose of health had to fade from many young human faces to blossom in the robes she wore, whose every sense had been most daintily feasted, and her whole life summed up in one long thought of self,— think of finding herself in the next life a spiritual leper, a walking pestilence, personified disease, a sloughing sore of this life which the spirit has to get rid of, an excrement of this life's selfishness at which all good spirits stop their noses and shudder when she comes near! Don't you think if she realized that as a fact in time, it would work more effectually than much preaching? The hell of the drunkard, the libidinous, the blood-thirsty, or gold-greedy soul, they tell us, is the burning of the old, devouring passion which was *not* quenched by the chills of death. The crossing of the cold, dark river, even, was only as the untasted water to the consuming thirst of Tantalus! In support of this, evolution shows the continuity of ourselves, our desires, passions and characters. As the Egyptians said, " Whoso is intelligent here will be intelligent there!" And if we haven't mastered and disciplined our lower passions here, they will be masters of us, for the time being, hereafter."

In lyric verse Gerald Massey ranks among the first English poets. His descriptions of humble life, portrayal of profoundly human sentiments, and exquisitely delicate reflections of those subtle emotions which are the common heritage of every true man and woman, have rarely been equalled. They reveal the power of the true poet. Take, for example, the following stanzas selected from " Babe Christabel," and note the purity, wealth of feeling

and beauty of expression which clothe the
simple story of dawn and night in the
human heart : —

Babe Christabel was royally born !
　　For when the earth was flushed with flowers,
　　And drenched with beauty in sunshowers,
She came through golden gates of morn.

No chamber arras-pictured round,
　　Where sunbeams make a gorgeous gloom,
　　And touch its glories into bloom,
And footsteps fall withouten sound,

Was her birth-place that merry May morn ;
　　No gifts were heaped, no bells were rung,
　　No healths were drunk, no songs were sung,
When dear Babe Christabel was born :

But nature on the darling smiled,
　　And with her beauty's blessings crowned :
　　Love brooded o'er the hallowed ground,
And there were angels with the child.

　　　　*　　　*　　　*　　　*　　　*　　　*

The father, down in toil's mirk mine,
    Turns to his wealthier world above,
    Its radiance, and its home of love ;
And lights his life like sun-struck wine.

The mother moves with queenlier tread :
    Proud swell the globes of ripe delight
    Above her heart, so warm and white
A pillow for the baby-head !

      *

She grew a sweet and sinless child,
    In shine and shower, calm and strife ;
    A rainbow on our dark of life,
From love's own radiant heaven down-smiled !

In lonely loveliness she grew,—
    A shape all music, light, and love,
    With startling looks, so eloquent of
The spirit whitening into view.

           *   *   *

And still her cheek grew pale as pearl,—
    It took no tint of summer's wealth
    Of color, warmth, and wine of health :
Death's hand so whitely pressed the girl !

No blush grew ripe to sun or kiss
  Where violet veins ran purple light,
  So tenderly through Parian white,
Touching you into tenderness.

 * * * * * *

She came — as comes the light of smiles
  O'er earth, and every budding thing
  Makes quick with beauty, alive with spring;
Then goeth to the golden isles.

She came — like music in the night
  Floating as heaven in the brain,
  A moment oped, and shut again,
And all is dark where all was light.

She thought our good-night kiss was given,
  And like a flower her life did close.
  Angels uncurtained that repose,
And the next waking dawned in heaven.

They snatched our little tenderling,
  So shyly opening into view,
  Delighted, as the children dc
The primrose that is first in spring

The lines quoted above are taken from various parts of the poem, and therefore do not present the unity of thought which characterizes the exquisite creation as a whole. "My Cousin Winnie" is another very charming poem, in which the author describes the child love which throbbed in his heart, when, as a boy, he basked in the smiles of "Cousin Winnie." I have space for a few stanzas only. They will be sufficient, however, to call up many long-vanished images to the mind of the reader. For the chambers of the human brain are stored with springtime treasures, which are forgotten until some magic word is spoken, some picture flashed upon the mental retina, or a sound of long ago is heard, and straightway the sealed door flies open, and forth come trooping, as children from a country school, the dreams and hopes which gilded life's young day : —

The glad spring green grows luminous
  With coming summer's golden glow;
Merry birds sing as they sang to us
  In far-off seasons, long ago:
The old place brings the young dawn back,
  That moist eyes mirror in their dew;
My heart goes forth along the track
  Where oft it danced, dear Winnie, with you.
A world of time, a sea of change,
  Have rolled between the paths we tread,
Since you were my " Cousin Winnie," and I
  Was your " own little, good little Ned."
  * * * * * *

My being in your presence basked,
  And kitten-like for pleasure purred;
A higher heaven I never asked
  Than watching, wistful as a bird,
To hear that voice so rich and low;
  Or sun me in the rosy rise
Of some soul-ripening smile, and know
  The thrill of opening paradise.
The boy might look too tenderly —
  All lightly 'twas interpreted:
You were my " Cousin Winnie," and I
  Was your " own little, good little Ned."
  * * * * * *

And then that other voice came in!
   There my life's music suddenly stopped.
Silence and darkness fell between
   Us, and my star from heaven dropped.
I led him by the hand to you —
   He was my friend — whose name you bear:
I had prayed for some great task to do,
   To prove my love. I did it, dear!
He was not jealous of poor me;
   Nor saw my life bleed under his tread:
You were my " Cousin Winnie," and I
   Was your " own little, good little Ned."

I smiled, dear, at your happiness —
   So martyrs smile upon the spears —
The smile of your reflected bliss
   Flashed from my heart's dark tarn of tears!
In love that made the suffering sweet,
   My blessing with the rest was given —
" God's softest flowers kiss her feet
   On earth, and crown her head in heaven!"

And lest the heart should leap to tell
   Its tale i' the eyes, I bowed the head:
You were my " Cousin Winnie," and I
   Was your " own little, good little Ned."
    *   *   *   *   *   *

Alone, unwearying, year by year,
   I go on laying up my love,
I think God makes no promise here
   But it shall be fulfilled above;
I think my wild weed of the waste
   Will one day prove a flower most sweet;
My love shall bear its fruit at last —
   'Twill all be righted when we meet;
And I shall find them gathered up
   In pearls for you — the tears I've shed
Since you were my " Cousin Winnie," and I
   Was your " own little, good little Ned."

Here again in " The Mother's Idol Broken " — which, in my judgment, is the finest work of this character written by Mr. Massey — we find a depth of emotion, a beauty of imagery, and a wealth of pure poetic power which would have done honor to Tennyson in the best moods of the late poet laureate.

After describing the mother's joy over the advent of the babe in the household, our poet continues : —

And proud ere her eyes as she rose with the
    prize,
A pearl in her palms, my peerless!

Oh, found you a little sea siren,
    In some perilous palace left?
· Or is it a little child angel,
    Of her high-born kin bereft?
Or came she out of the elfin land,
    By earthly love beguiled?
Or hath the sweet spirit of beauty
    Taken shape as our starry child?

With mystical faint fragrance,
    Our house of life she filled —
Revealed each hour some fairy tower,
    Where wingèd hopes might build.

We saw — though none like us might see —
    Such precious promise pearled
Upon the petals of our wee
    White Rose of all the world!

*   ⁒   *   *   *

Our Rose was but in blossom;
    Our life was but in spring;

When down the solemn midnight
  We heard the spirits sing :
" *Another bud of infancy,*
  With holy dews impearled,"
And in their hands they bore our wee
  White Rose of all the world.

She came like April, who with tender grace
Smiles in earth's face, and sets upon her breast
The bud of all her glory yet to come,
Then bursts in tears, and takes her sorrowful leave.
She brought heaven to us just within the space
Of the dear depths of her large, dream-like eyes,
Then o'er the vista fell the death-veil dark.
She only caught three words of human speech :
One for her mother, one for me, and one
She crowed with, for the fields and open air.
That last she sighed with a sharp farewell pathos
A minute ere she left the house of life,
To come for kisses never any more.

Pale Blossom ! how she leaned in love to us !
And how we feared a hand might reach from
      heaven
To pluck our sweetest flower, our loveliest flower

Of life, that sprang from lowliest root of love !
Some tender trouble in her eyes complained
Of Life's rude stream, as meek forget-me-nots
Make sweet appeal when winds and waters fret.
And oft she looked beyond us with sad eyes,
As for the coming of the Unseen Hand.
We saw ,but feared to speak of, her strange beauty,
As some hushed bird that dares not sing i' the
    night,
Lest lurking foe should find its secret place,
And seize it through the dark. With twin-love's
    strength
All crowded in the softest nestling-touch,
We fenced her round,—exchanging silent looks.
We went about the house with listening hearts,
That kept the watch for danger's stealthiest step.
Our spirits felt the shadow ere it fell.

    *   *   *   *   *

The mornings came with all their glory on ;
Birds, brooks, and bees were singing in the sun,
Earth's blithe heart breathing bloom into her face,
The flowers all crowding up like memories
Of lovelier life in some forgotten world,
Or dreams of peace and beauty yet to come.
The soft south-breezes rocked the baby-buds

In fondling arms upon a balmy breast;
And all was gay as universal life
Swam down the stream that glads the City of God.

But we lay dark where Death had struck us down
With that stern blow which made us bleed within,
And bow while the Inevitable went by.

    *   *   *   *   *   *

This is a curl of little Marian's hair!
A ring of sinless gold that weds two worlds!

Poetic genius of a high order is displayed in this remarkable production, and though the extracts given above carry with them the spirit of the poem, they are only threads in what, when taken as a whole, is a cloth of many tints, rich in color and fine in texture.

Seldom do we find anything so pure and sweet as the following lines taken from "Wedded Love," in which the poet gives us a glimpse of his own deep and rich experiences : —

My life ran like a river in rocky ways,
And seaward dashed, a sounding cataract!
But thine was like a quiet lake of beauty,
Soft-shadowed round by gracious influences,
That gathers silently its wealth of earth,
And woos heaven till it melts down into it.

They mingled: and the glory and the calm
Closed round me, brooding into perfect rest.
Oh, blessings on thy true and tender heart!
How it hath gone forth like the dove of old,
To bring some leaf of promise in life's deluge!
Thou hast a strong up-soaring tendency,
That bears me Godward, as the stalwart oak
Uplifts the clinging vine, and gives it growth.
Thy reverent heart familiarly doth take
Unconscious clasp of high and holy things,
And trusteth where it may not understand.
We have had sorrows, love! and wept the tears
That run the rose-hue from the cheeks of life;
But grief hath jewels as night hath her stars,
And she revealeth what we ne'er had known,
With joy's wreath tumbled o'er our blinded eyes.
The heart is like an instrument whose strings
Steal nobler music from life's many frets;

The golden threads are spun through suffering's
    fire,
Wherewith the marriage robes for heaven are
    woven;
And all the rarest hues of human life
Take radiance, and are rainbowed out in tears.

Thou'rt little changed, dear love! since we were
    wed.
Thy beauty hath climaxed like a crescent moon,
With glory greatening to the golden full.
Thy flowers of spring are crowned with summer
    fruits,
And thou hast put a queenlier presence on
With thy regality of womanhood!
Yet time but toucheth thee with mellowing shades
That set thy graces in a wealthier light.
Thy soul still looks with its rare smile of love,
From the gate beautiful of its palace home,
Fair as the spirit of the evening star,
That lights its glory as a radiant porch
To beacon earth with brighter glimpse of heaven.
We are poor in this world's wealth, but rich in
    love;
And they who love feel rich in everything.

    *   *   *   *   *   *

Oh, let us walk the world, so that our love
Burn like a blessed beacon, beautiful
Upon the walls of life's surrounding dark.
Ah! what a world 'twould be if love like ours
Made heaven in human hearts, and clothed with
  smiles
The sweet, sad face of our humanity!

In "The Young Poet to His Wife" are
many fine lines, perhaps none more beautiful than the following : —

O, Love will make the killing crown of thorn
Burst into blossom on the Martyr's brow!
Upon Love's bosom Earth floats like an Ark
Through all the o'erwhelming deluge of the night.
Love rays us round as glory swathes a star,
And from the mystic touch of lips and palms,
Streams rosy warmth enough to light a world.

Among Mr. Massey's personal poems
his tribute to the author of "The Song
of the Shirt," is by far the finest. Indeed,
this poem is a superb production. The
melancholy spectacle of Hood battling

with disease, bravely editing his magazine and composing immortal lines while confined to his bed and racked with pain was enough to appeal to the imagination and sympathy of a large-hearted nature like Gerald Massey's. And then these two champions of the poor were kindred souls. He who wrote " The Bridge of Sighs " was naturally endeared to the poet who penned " The Cry of the Unemployed." Hood was worthy of the following tribute, which I regard as among the finest specimens of Massey's work : —

'Twas the old story ! — ever the blind world
Knows not its Angels of Deliverance
Till they stand glorified 'twixt earth and heaven.
It stones the Martyr ; then, with praying hands,
Sees the God mount his chariot of fire,
And calls sweet names, and worships what it
    spurned.
It slays the Man to deify the Christ :
And then how lovingly 'twill bind the brows

Where late its thorn-crown laughed with cruel
   lips —
Red, and rejoicing from the killing kiss !
To those who walk beside them, great men seem
Mere common earth; but distance makes them
   stars.
As dying limbs do lengthen out in death,
So grows the stature of their after-fame ;
And then we gather up their glorious words,
And treasure up their names with loving care.
So Hood, our Poet, lived his martyr-life ;
With a swift soul that travelled at such speed,
And struck such flashes from its flinty road,
That by its trail of radiance through the dark,
We almost see the unfeatured Future's face,—
And went uncrowned to his untimely tomb.
'Tis true, the world did praise his glorious wit —
The merry Jester with his cap and bells !
And sooth, his wit was like Ithuriel's spear ;
But 'twas mere lightening from the cloud of his
   life,
Which held at heart most rich and blessed rain
Of tear's melodious, that are worlds of love ;
And Rainbows that would bridge from earth to
   heaven ;
And Light, that should have shone like Joshua's sun

Above our long death-grapple with the Wrong;
And thunder-voices, with their Words of fire,
To melt the slaves chain, and the Tyrant's crown.
His wit? — a kind smile just to hearten us ! —
Rich foam-wreaths on the waves of lavish life,
That flashed o'er precious pearls and golden sands.
But, there was that beneath surpassing wit !ˊ
The starry soul, that shines when all is dark ! —
Endurance, that can suffer and grow strong —
Walk through the world with bleeding feet, and
    smile ! —
Love's inner light, that kindles Life's rare colours,
Bright wine of Beauty for the longing soul ;
And thoughts that swathe Humanity with such
    glory
As lines the outline of the coming God.
In him were gleams of such heroic splendour
As light this cold, dark world up like a star
Arrayed in glory for the eyes of heaven :
And a great heart that beat according music
With theirs of old, — God-likest kings of men!
A conquering heart! which Circumstance, that
    frights
The many down from Love's transfiguring height,
Aye mettled into martial attitude.
He might have clutched the palm of Victory

In the world's wrestling-ring of noble deeds;
But he went down a precious Argosy
At sea, just glimmering into sight of shore,
With its rare freightage from diviner climes.
While friends were crowding at the Harbour mouth
To meet and welcome the brave Sailor back,
He saw, and sank in sight of them at home!
The world may never know the wealth it lost,
When Hood went darkling to his tearful tomb,
So mighty in his undeveloped force!
With all his crowding unaccomplished hopes —
Th' unuttered wealth and glory of his soul —
And all the music ringing round his life,
And poems stirring in his dying brain.
But blessings on him for the songs he sang —
Which yearned about the world till then for birth!
How like a bonny bird of God he came,
And poured his heart in music for the Poor;
Who sit in gloom while sunshine floods the land,
And grope through darkness, for the hand of Help.
And trampled Manhood heard, and claimed its
        crown;
And trampled Womanhood sprang up ennobled!
The human soul looked radiantly through rags!
And there was melting of cold hearts, as when
The ripening sunlight fingers frozen flowers.

O ! blessings on him for the songs he sang !
When all the stars of happy thought had set
In many a mind, his spirit walked the gloom
Clothed on with beauty, as the regal Moon
Walks her night-kingdom, turning clouds to light.
Our Champion ! with his heart too big to beat
In bonds,— our Poet in his pride of power !
Aye, we'll remember him who fought our fight,
And chose the Martyr's robe of flame, and spurned
The gold and purple of the glistering slave.
His Mausoleum is the People's heart,
There he lies crowned and glorified,— in state.

Many of Europe's most competent and
conscientious critics have expressed their
appreciation of the high order of much of
Mr. Massey's poetical work. " I rejoice,"
wrote John Ruskin to the poet, " in ac-
knowledging my own debt of gratitude to
you for many an encouraging and noble
thought, and expression of thought. Few
national services can be greater than that
you have rendered." Thomas Aird, in
a critical review, observed: " Gerald

Massey belongs to the new choir. Pathos and love and a purple flush of beauty steep the color of all his songs." The eminent essayist, Walter Bagehot, in criticising Mr. Massey's work, said : " His descriptions of nature show a close observer of her ways, and a delicate appreciation of her beauties. His images, however subtle and delicately woven, are never false."

Here are some melodious stanzas which tell us of the poet's hope for a brighter tomorrow, a hope which he entertained before his long and careful psychical investigation, led to the positive conviction expressed in his later prose and poetical works :

Although its features fade in light of unimagined
    bliss,
We have shadowy revealings of the Better World
    in this :

A little glimpse, when Spring unveils her face and
    opes her eyes,
Of the Sleeping Beauty in the soul that wakes in
    Paradise.

A little drop of Heaven in each diamond of the
    shower,
A breath of the Eternal in the fragrance of each
    flower!

A little low vibration in the warble of Night's bird,
Of the praises and the music that shall be hereafter
    heard!

A little whisper in the leaves that clap their hands
    and try
To glad the heart of man, and lift to Heaven his
    grateful eye.

A little semblance mirrored in old Ocean's smile or
    frown
Of His vast glory who doth bow the Heavens and
    come down!

A little symbol shining through the worlds that
    move at rest
On invisible foundations of the broad Almighty
    breast!

A little hint that stirs and thrills the wings we fold
within,
And tells of that full heaven yonder which must
here begin !

A little springlet welling from the fountain head
above,
That takes its earthly way to find the ocean of
all love !

A little silver shiver in the ripple of the river
Caught from the light that knows no night forever
and forever !

A little hidden likeness, often faded or defiled,
Of the great, the good All-father, in His poorest
human child !

Although the best be lost in light of unimagined
bliss,
We have shadowy revealings of the Better World
in this.

As I have said before, there is little
doubt but that Gerald Massey would have
become one of England's most famous lyric
poets, had he chosen to confine his gifts to

subjects pleasing to wealth and convention-alism; but, like other royal souls, who throughout the past have persistently held to the path of duty, he chose to be loyal to truth and faithful to earth's oppressed, ever preferring the bread of poverty with the approval of his higher self, to the applause of the *dilettanti* with a life of comparative ease. Such spirits are rarely appreciated until they have passed from earth. They belong to the Royalty of Nature; they are in truth the Sons of God.

"*Immortal Liberty, we see thee stand,*
Like morn just stepped from heaven, upon a mountain."

THE reformer is always the possible prophet. He whose nature is so finely strung and whose conscience so sensitive to the eternal verities as they relate to right and wrong that he feels injuries inflicted upon the unfortunate and injustice practised upon the defenceless as though the evil fell upon himself, sustains an intimate relationship to the highest as well as the humblest expressions of life. If the cry of the wretch under the wheel wrings his heart, he is also soothed by divine symphonies, which those of duller sensibilities are unconscious of; and upon his spiritual perception there frequently flash the lights and shadows of the coming morrow. It was thus with the great prophets of Israel. It was thus with John Huss and Savonarola. It was thus with Whittier and Wendell Phillips. And it is thus, in a very marked degree, with Gerald Massey.

It is something more than an unconquerable faith in the ultimate triumph of good, learned from the slow ascent of man, that inspires the following thrilling lines, which are peculiarly appropriate to our present social conditions, when a new-born sense of right and a quickened intelligence are leading millions throughout civilization to demand a fairer share in the bounties of life : —

Immortal liberty! we see thee stand
   Like morn just stepped from heaven upon a
     mountain
With beautiful feet, and blessing-laden hand,
   And heart that welleth love's most living fountain!
Oh, when wilt thou draw from the people's lyre
   Joy's broken cord? and on the people's brow

Set empire's crown? light up thine altar-fire
  Within their hearts, with an undying glow;
Nor give us blood for milk, as men are drunk with
    now?

Old legends tell us of a golden age,
  When earth was guiltless — gods the guests of
    men,
Ere sin had dimmed the heart's illumined page,—
  And prophet-voices say 'twill come again,
O happy age! when love shall rule the heart,
  And time to live shall be the poor man's dower,
When martyrs bleed no more, nor exiles smart —
  Mind is the only diadem of power.
People, it ripens now! Awake, and strike the hour!

Hearts, high and mighty, gather in our cause;
  Bless, bless, O God, and crown their earnest labor,
Who dauntless fight to win us equal laws,
  With mental armor and with spirit sabre!
Bless, bless, O God! the proud intelligence,
  That now is dawning on the people's forehead,—
Humanity springs from them like incense,
  The future bursts upon them, boundless, star-
    ried —
They weep repentant tears, that they so long have
    tarried.

The spiritual intuition or perception of the true prophet soul was beautifully expressed in the legend of the despairing sage. The story comes from that far-away time when types and symbols were used by the children of earth, and when man was so near to nature that at times he seemed to hear the voice of the Creator.

The sage, so runs the story, had toiled for his fellow-men through years of suffering and privation. He had closed his eyes against the temptations of luxury and ease which were held out to lure him from the service of his race. He had dwelt with poverty and had nursed the plague-stricken, had fed the starving, always striving to fix the eyes of his fellow-men upon that which was enduring and divine. He reasoned with scholars on the higher philosophy of life, and strove to impress upon them the kinship of mankind. He appealed to the rich to be just, and boldly assailed tyranny and oppression. Often he had to fly from city to city, and sometimes he was offered great bribes to hold his peace. But neither the threat of power nor the bribe of wealth swerved him from his course. His all-consuming desire was to bring about the realization of the dream which haunted his soul. He longed to behold justice, peace and love blossom among the children of men.

At length he became a very old man; his hair was silvered, his face bronzed and furrowed, his step halting and feeble. Many who had followed him when he had been able to minister to their physical needs now fell away, and the seeds he had planted seemed to have rotted and died. One day he sought the solitude of the moutains and in bitterness of soul prayed that he might die; in his depression of spirit it seemed to him that he had lived in vain, and the future appeared to be in the possession of the powers of darkness. Virtue, love and peace seemed routed all along the line of human endeavor.

While lost in prayer, so runs this legend, the sage became overcome with a sense of peace known only to the victor in a glorious cause. Then the heaviness of earth fell away; his soul entered an ecstatic condition; his spirit was borne aloft in a chariot of luminous clouds upheld and guided by invisible hands. At length his eyes were opened, when lo! he was encompassed by a multitude of radiant souls. Then his ears caught the symphony of nature; he was bewildered. The multitudes around him were incarnations of light, of purity, of love and wisdom. They were victors, and the music which swelled upon the ear was an anthem of triumph.

An angel of lofty mien appeared, saying: "Because of the failing power of the physical form, the truth has become veiled to thy vision. Now behold the work of thy life."

Then to him was given the power of the Universal Eye. He beheld a home where now dwelt a father, once a plague-stricken boy nursed by the sage. The father sang to his son the songs of love, courage and brotherhood which he had learned from the prophet long years ago. In another cottage he beheld a mother telling the story of the great man whose life made all men better, and through whose loving care the mother was then alive. And he noted the radiance in the faces of the eager children as they exclaimed, " We want to be like him ! "

Then he beheld one whom he had taught in years gone by discoursing to a vast multitude upon the truths which the prophet had in former days impressed upon his brain. He saw thousands of eager ears strained to hear the evangel which fell from the eloquent lips of one he had known as a ragged boy, who had followed him from village to village with other poor people. And then the panorama broadened, until he beheld that he had all unconsciously kindled fires for truth which should yet illuminate his people.

Then the angel said, " Look once more," and he beheld the tumult of battle, he heard the screams of the multitude, who sank on every hand. After the battle came injustice and oppression; he heard the cry of those under the oppressor and beheld the sufferings of the world; and as in horror he sought the angel's face, a light dawned. It came from the hearts and homes of the multitudes. Then the light grew brighter; it spread from hut to cottage, from cottage to palace. A new conflict was in progress. Man met man in a struggle on a higher plane; ideas were weapons more often than swords, and in

the dim future the sage saw the whole
world bathed in the light of justice, man-
tled in peace and prosperity.

So it is with the reformers of all times.
At moments their souls, so sensitive and
responsive to the suffering and misery of
life, also catch the strains of the higher
music. Their eyes, which see the suffering
of the unfortunate and the poor as though
every trial was their own, also at intervals
catch glimpses of the coming day. In
one of these great visions Gerald Massey
breaks into the following triumphant
strain :

’ Tis coming up the steep of time,
   And this old world is growing brighter !
We may not see its dawn sublime,
   Yet high hopes make the heart throb lighter !
Our dust may slumber under ground
   When it awakes the world in wonder ;
But we have felt it gathering round —
   Have heard its voice of distant thunder !
     ’ Tis coming ! yes, ’tis coming !

'Tis coming now, that glorious time
  Foretold by seers and sung in story,
For which, when thinking was a crime,
  Souls leaped to heaven from scaffolds gory !
They passed.   But lo ! the work they wrought !
  Now the crowned hopes of centuries blossom ;
The lightning of their living thought
  Is flashing through us, brain and bosom :
    'Tis coming ! yes, 'tis coming !

Creeds, empires, systems, rot with age,
  But the great people's ever youthful !
And it shall write the future's page
  To our humanity more truthful ;
There's a divinity within
  That makes men great if they but will it ,
God works with all who dare to win,
  And the time cometh to reveal it.
    ' Tis coming ! yes, ' tis coming !

Fraternity ! Love's other name !
  Dear, heaven-connecting link of being ;
Then shall we grasp thy golden dream,
  As souls, full-statured, grow far-seeing :
Thou shalt unfold our better part,
  And in our life cup yield more honey ;

Light up with joy the poor man's heart,
  And love's own world with smiles more sunny!
    'Tis coming! yes, 'tis coming!

Jesus, who was the supreme expression of love, was terrible in His denunciations when confronted by the hypocrisy and selfishness of slothful, self-indulgent conventionalism. Gerald Massey has penned some of the sweetest lines ever written by poet of the people, but when he faces the plunderers of the toiling millons, when he looks upon the hypocrite and oppressor, he becomes transformed. His words are no longer soothing and peaceful; the limpid brook becomes a roaring torrent. The voice which speaks in the following lines is not the voice of one man, but the articulate cry of millions, thrown into speech by the instrument of God, that the wise may be warned, and, being warned, may be saved from the ruin which must and will overtake that society which selfishly imag-

ines it can eternally thwart the upward
march of humanity : —

Back, tramplers on the many! Death **and** danger
    ambushed lie ;
Beware ye, or the blood may run! The patient
    people cry :
" Ah, shut not out the light of hope, or we may
    blindly dash,
Like Samson with his strong death-grope, and whelm
    ye in the crash.
Think how they spurred the people **mad**, that old
    regime of France,
Whose heads, like poppies, from death's scythe, fell
    in a bloody dance.

In the following stanzas we are reminded of some of the old prophets of
Israel, who championed the cause of God
and the poor at the risk of life, and uttered
luminous truths which still light up man's
pathway. Mr. Massey is nothing if not a
fearless reformer. He does not believe in
a half loaf when justice is the issue. The

people have certain rights of which they are deprived by the special privileges enjoyed by a favored few. Against these wrongs, which are day by day becoming more apparent to thoughtful and truly enlightened men and women, our poet speaks with that courage and sincerity which is as refreshing as it is rare in our age of sycophancy : —

Thus saith the Lord : You weary me
    With prayers, and waste your own short years;
Eternal truth you cannot see
    Who weep, and shed your sight in tears !
In vain you wait and watch the skies —
    No better fortune thus will fall ;
Up from your knees I bid you rise,
    And claim the earth for all.

Behold in bonds your mother earth,
    The rich man's prostitute and slave !
Your mother earth, that gave you birth,
    You only *own* her for a grave !
And will you die like slaves, and see
    Your mother left a fettered thrall !

Nay live like men and set her free
  As heritage for all.

In the same strain, and speaking not as
an individual but as the articulate voice of
eternal justice, Mr. Massey elsewhere utters
these words to the toiling millions : —

Lift up your faces from the sod ;
  Frown with each furrowed brow ;
Gold apes a mightier power than God,
  And wealth is worshipped now !
In all these toil-ennobled lands
  You have no heritage ;
They snatch the fruit of youthful hands,
  The staff from weary age.
Oh, tell them in their palaces,
  These lords of land and money,
They shall not kill the poor like bees,
  To rob them of life's honey.

Through long, dark years of blood and tears,
  You've toiled like branded slaves
Till wrong's red hand hath made a land
  Of paupers, prisons, graves !

But our long sufferance endeth now ;
　　Within the souls of men
The fruitful buds of promise blow,
　　And freedom lives again !
Oh, tell them in their palaces,
　　These lords of land and money,
They shall not kill the poor like bees,
　　To rob them of life's honey.

In his prose works he takes the same radical and uncompromising stand for absolute justice for the lowliest. In one place he says : —

" We mean to have a day of reckoning with the unjust stewards of the earth. We mean to have the national property restored to the people. We mean that the land, with its inalienable right of living, its mineral wealth below the soil and its waters above, shall be open to all. We mean to have our banking done by the state, and our railways worked for the benefit of the whole people. We mean to temper the terror of rampart individualism with the principles of co-operation. We mean for woman to have perfect equality with man, social, religous and political, and her fair share in that equity which is of no sex. We mean also that the same standard of morality shall apply to the man as to the woman. In short, we intend that the redress of wrongs and the righting of inequalities, which can only be rectified in this world, shall not be put off and postponed to any future stage of existence."

In another place he asserts with emphasis : —

"*Humanity is one.* The Eternal intends to show us that *humanity* is *one.* And the family is more than the individual member, the Nation is more than the family, and the human race is more than the nation. And if we do not accept the revelation lovingly, do not take to the fact kindly, why then 'tis flashed upon us terribly, by lightning of hell, if we will not have it by light of heaven — and the poor, neglected scum and *canaille* of the nations rise up mighty in the strength of disease, and prove the oneness of humanity by killing you with the same infection.

"It has recently been shown how the poor of London do not live, but fester in the pestilential hovels called their homes. To get into these you have to visit courts which the sun never penetrates, which are never visited by a breath of fresh air, and which never know the virtues of a drop of cleansing water. Immorality is but the natural outcome of such a devil's spawning ground. The poverty of many who strive to live honestly is appalling.

"And this disclosure is made with the customary moan that such people attend neither church nor chapel, as if that were the panacea. I should not wonder if these revelations result in the building of more churches and chapels, and the consecration of at least one or two more bishops.

"The Bishop of Bedford said the other day, ' It was highly necessary that in these times when the poor have so little earthly enjoyment, the joys of heaven should be made known to them.' It is not possible to caricature an utterance so grotesque as that."

In his songs of humanity, there is the calm assurance of the philosopher, that right will ultimately prevail. He pleads for the millions under the rod. He may not see the false falling away around him, but far up the mountain slope he sees the purpling dawn growing brighter. Looking backward he perceives that the present, with its hideousness and wrong is not, so dark as the past, and with that trust in the final triumph of right which makes him optimistic, he thus refers to his songs for the oppressed : —

Let my songs be cited
  As breakers of the peace,
Till the wrongs are righted,
  The man-made miseries cease;
Till earth's disinherited
Beg no more to earn their bread;
Till the consuming darts of burning day
Shall fire the midnight foxes; scare away
From labor's fruits the parasites of prey.
  Let them die when all is done,
  Now victoriously begun!
Our visions have not come to naught,
  Who saw by lightning in the night,
The deeds we dreamed are being wrought
  By those who work in clearer light;
In other ways our fight is fought,
And other forms fulfill our thought
  Made visible to all men's sight.

There is a certain thought-compelling
power in many of his poems of labor found
only in the work of an enthusiast, mad
with divine love for his fellow-men. Often
he outlines upon his canvas a splendid
dream, a big hope, a grand aspiration, and

then in the foreground he paints with a few bold strokes a frightful truth. The antithesis is tremendous in its effects, as will be seen in the following stanza : —

When the heart of one-half the world doth beat
  Akin to the brave and the true,
And the tramp of democracy's earth-quaking feet
  Goes thrilling the wide world through—
We should not be crouching in darkness and dust,
  And dying like slaves in the night;
But big with the might of the inward " *must* "
  We should battle for freedom and right!
Our fathers are praying for pauper pay,
  Our mothers with death's kiss are white;
Our sons are the rich man's serfs by day,
  And our daughters his slaves by night.

Many of Massey's poems are as applicable to the problems now confronting us as if called forth by present-day conditions in our own land. Take for example the following " Cry of the Unemployed," which reveals the profound sympathy and appreciation felt by our poet for the struggling unfortunates :—

'Tis hard to be a wanderer through this bright
    world of ours,
Beneath a sky of smiling blue, on fragrant paths of
    flowers,
With music in the woods, as there were nought but
    pleasure known,
Or Angels walked Earth's solitudes, and yet with
    want to groan :
To see no beauty in the stars, nor in Earth's wel-
    come smile,
To wander cursed with misery ! willing, but cannot
    toil.
With burning sickness at my heart, I sink down
    famished :
God of the Wretched, hear my prayer : I would that
    I were dead !

Heaven droppeth down with manna still in many a
    golden shower,
And feeds the leaves with fragrant breath, with
    silver dew the flower.
Honey and fruit for Bee and Bird, with bloom
    laughs out the tree,

And food for all God's happy things; but none
  gives food to me.
Earth, wearing plenty for a crown, smiles on my
  aching eye,
The purse-proud, — swathed in luxury, — disdainful
  pass me by:
I've willing hands, and eager heart — but may not
  work for bread!
God of the Wretched, hear my prayer: I would
  that I were dead!

Gold, art thou not a blessed thing, a charm above
  all other,
To shut up hearts to Nature's cry, when brother
  pleads with brother?
Hast thou a music sweeter than the voice of loving
  kindness?
No! curse thee, thou'rt a mist 'twixt God and men
  in outer blindness.
"*Father, come back*"! my Children cry; their
  voices, once so sweet,
Now pierce and quiver in my heart! I cannot, dare
  not meet
The looks that make the brain go mad, for dear
  ones asking bread —
God of the Wretched, hear my prayer: I would
  that I were dead!

Lord! what right have the poor to wed? Love's
    for the gilded great:
Are they not formed of nobler clay, who dine off
    golden plate?
'Tis the worst curse of Poverty to have a feeling
    heart:
Why can I not, with iron grasp, choke out the
    tender part?
I cannot slave in yon Bastille! I think 'twere
    bitterer pain,
To wear the Pauper's iron within, than drag the
    Convict's chain.
I'd work but cannot, starve I may, but will not beg
    for bread:
God of the Wretched, hear my prayer: I would
    that I were dead!

The slow progress of justice frequently
makes the faint-hearted waver, and many
who start out in youth brave and valiant
reformers are lured into the toils of slothful conventionalism, others become des-
pondent and give up even before the sun
of life has crossed the meridian. To such

faltering ones Gerald Massey speaks in these stirring lines : —

Never despair! O, my Comrades in sorrow!
  I know that our mourning is ended not. Yet,
Shall the vanquished today be the Victors tomor-
    row.
  Our star shall shine on in the Tyrant's Sunset.
Hold on! though they spurn thee, for whom thou
    art living
  A life only cheered by the lamp of its love.
Hold on! Freedom's hope to the bounden ones
    giving;
  Green spots in the waste wait the worn spirit-
    dove.
Hold on, — still hold on, — in the world's despite,
  Nurse the faith in thy heart, keep the lamp of
    Truth bright,
And, my life for thine! it shall end in the Right.

What, though the Martyrs and Prophets have per-
    ished!
  The Angel of Life rolls the stone from their
    graves:
Immortal's the faith and the freedom they cher-
    ished,
  Their lone Triumph-cry stirs the spirits of slaves!

They are gone, — but a Glory is left in our life,
  Like the day-god's last kiss on the darkness of
    Even –
Gone down on the desolate seas of their strife,
  To climb as star-beacons up Liberty's heaven.
Hold on, — still hold on, — in the world's despite
  Nurse the faith in thy heart, keep the lamp of
    Truth bright,
And, my life for thine ! it shall end in the Right.

Think of the Wrongs that have ground us for ages,
  Think of the Wrongs we have still to endure !
Think of our blood, red on History's pages ;
  Then work that our reck'ning be speedy and sure.
Slaves cry to their Gods ! but be our God revealed
  In our lives, in our words, in our warfare for
    man ;
And bearing — or borne upon — Victory's shield,
  Let us fight battle-harnessed, and fall in the van.
Hold on, — still hold on, — in the world's despite,
  Nurse the faith in thy heart, keep the lamp of
    Truth bright,
And, my life for thine ! it shall end in the Right.

And to the faint heart who would turn
aside because the multitude fail to appre-

ciate the single-hearted struggle made for them, our poet has this message : —

Hope on, hope ever ! though To-day be dark,
    The sweet sunburst may smile on thee Tomorrow ;
Though thou art lonely, there's an eye will mark
    Thy loneliness, and guerdon all thy sorrow ?
Though thou must toil 'mong cold and sordid men,
    With none to echo back thy thought, or love
      thee,
Cheer up, poor heart ! thou dost not beat in vain
    While God is over all, and heaven above thee,
        Hope on, hope ever,

The iron may enter in and pierce the soul,
    But cannot kill the love within thee burning,
The tears of misery, thy bitter dole,
    Can never quench thy true heart's eager yearn-
      ing
For better things ; nor crush thy ardour's trust,
    That Error from the mind shall be uprooted,
That Truth shall flower from all this tear-dewed
    dust,
    And Love be cherished where Hate was em-
    bruted !
        Hope on, hope ever.

I know 'tis hard to bear the sneer and taunt,—
  With the heart's honest pride at midnight wres-
    tle;
To feel the killing canker-worm of Want
  While rich rogues in their mocking luxury nestle;
For I have felt it. Yet from Earth's cold Real
  My soul looks out on coming things, and cheerful
The warm Sunrise floods all the land Ideal,
  And still it whispers to the worn and tearful,
      Hope on, hope ever.

Hope on, hope ever! after darkest night
  Comes full of loving life, the laughing Morning;
Hope on, hope ever! Spring-tide, flushed with
    light,
  Aye crowns old Winter with her adorning.
Hope on, hope ever! For the time shall come,
  When man to man shall be a friend and brother;
And this old world shall be a happy home,
  And all Earth's family love one another!
      Hope on, hope ever.

In this little poem, entitled "The Kingliest Kings," the poet makes the same
stirring appeal to the conscience of the
individual : —

Ho! ye who in noble work
　　Win scorn, as flames draw air,
And in the way where Lions lurk,
　　God's image bravely bear;
Though trouble-tried and torture-torn,
The kingliest Kings are crowned with thorn.

Life's glory like the bow in heaven,
　　Still springeth from the cloud;
Soul ne'er out-soared the starry Seven
　　But Pain's fire-chariot rode:
They've battled best who've boldliest borne;
The kingliest Kings are crowned with thorn.

The martyr's fire-crown on the brow
　　Doth into glory burn;
And tears that from Love's torn heart flow,
　　To pearls of spirit turn,
Our dearest hopes in pangs are born;
The kingliest Kings are crowned with thorn.

As beauty in Death's cerement shrouds,
　　And Stars bejewel Night,
Bright thoughts are born in dim heart-clouds,
　　And suffering worketh might.
The mirkest hour is Mother o' Morn,
The kingliest Kings are crowned with thorn.

Such work is very effective. It gives the glorious ideal to which the noblest of earth's children aspire, and then it turns the flash-light upon the heinous crimes which easy-going conventionalism tolerates. The reformer beholds the wrong in all its enormity. He utters a cry of horror. The slow-thinking people are aroused by the cry, and they ask, Can such things be? They raise the question, and an agitation is commenced which, sooner or later, ends in victory for justice. The exclamation and interrogation points are the staff and crook of progress. I shall close my extracts from Mr. Massey's inspiring songs of labor by giving two stanzas from " The Awakening ":—

Oh! earth has no sight half so glorious to see,
As a people up-girding its might to be free.

To see men awake from the slumber of ages,
   Their brows grim from labor, their hands hard
      and tan,

Start up living heroes, long dreamt-of by Sages!
   And smite with strong arm the oppressors of
      man:
To see them come dauntless forth 'mid the world's
      warring,
   Slaves of the midnight mine! Serfs of the sod!
Show how the Eternal within them is stirring,
   And never more bend to a crownèd clod:
Dear God! 'tis a sight for Immortals to see,—
A People up-girding its might to be free.

Battle on bravely, O sons of Humanity!
   Dash down the cup from your lips, O ye Toilers!
Too long hath the world bled for Tyrant's insanity—
   Too long our weakness been strength to our
      spoilers!
The heart that through danger and death will be
      dutiful,
   Soul that with Cranmer in fire would shake
      hands,
And a life like a palace home built for the beauti-
      ful,
   Freedom of all her belovèd demands —
And earth has no sight half so glorious to see,
As People up-girding its might to be free!

Mr. Massey has labored throughout his life for the oppressed in every condition of ignorance and superstition. Wherever man, woman, or child has suffered through injustice, his voice has leaped forth in defence of the wronged, and against the wrong-doer he has waged an incessant warfare. He has boldly championed the cause of woman, steadfastly'demanding for her that full-orbed justice which she must receive before the higher civilization will be assured. And in the nineteenth century no philosopher or reformer has pleaded more earnestly for the rights of children, and that their lives be permitted to unfold under the best possible conditions, than this pure-souled, earnest man.

We are entering a struggle which will prove the most momentous Western civilization has ever known, because the conflict is along every line of advance. Social and economic problems, or the theory of man's relationship to man and to society as a whole; the problem of religion, the realm of psychical science, the rights of woman, the requirements and possibilities of childhood — these are some of the questions around which the forces of conservatism and progress are already rallying for a sanguinary conflict. Upon all these questions Mr. Massey has spoken, and spoken in no uncertain voice. And, what is more important, he has always placed himself squarely on the side of progress and the dawn. Therefore I believe that the generation of the future, who will enjoy, in a measure, the fruits of the higher and truer life for which the prophet worked, will appreciate his splendid services, and enshrine his name among the immortal *coterie* who placed truth and the good of their fellow-men above the comforts of life or the applause of the world.

THE prophet and mystic must not be confused with the priest, for, speaking broadly, the two represent widely divergent spheres of thought. The prophet is the herald of progress. He assails outgrown beliefs, entrenched wrongs, and conventional injustice. He points from the half truths which were once helpful stepping stones, but which now retard man's onward march, to the broader vision which the future presents. His eye rests on the luminous peaks which lie before. He has unbounded faith in freedom. He is often a destroyer of the old, but it is that the new may rise in fairer forms and be of more enduring character. If he tears down the log cabin, it is that he may erect the marble palace.

The priest, on the other hand, is the defender of conservatism. He distrusts the new. To him the prophet is a destructionist who ignores that which age has sanctified and time made venerable. He fears that wider liberty and greater knowledge will prove dangerous. He worships at the shrine of the past. What is written, or what other ages have believed, is, in a certain way, sacred to him. The question, Is it true? breaks powerless as waves before the precipice, when it beats against his prejudice and the veneration with which he views the established order which has been sanctified by time. The priest is the bulwark of conventionalism.

This contrast is strikingly illustrated in the history of Israel's prophets. But nowhere does it find so impressive an illustration as in the life of Jesus. Here we see the relative attitude of the two great spheres of thought represented by these classes. On the one side was Jesus, the prophet and mystic; on the other, the priesthood, upholding the past and defending conditions as they existed. Jesus cried, "Ye have heard it said, 'An eye for an eye,' but I say, Love your enemies." Jesus disregarded the ceremonials, the dogmas, and the forms held sacred by the church. He was a Sabbath breaker. He mingled with publicans and sinners. He healed the sick in a way entirely irregular. His teachings were regarded as sacrilegious and essentially dangerous to the established order. The great prophet and mystic pointed to the higher altitudes of spiritual attainment. He drew inspiration from the lily of the field. The gold of morning and the flaming scarlet of the evening, the stars and blue Galilee, spoke more eloquently to him of his Father than did the stories of bloody strife in which the God of love was represented as ordering defenceless women and innocent babes to be mercilessly slain. The priesthood then, as has been ever the case, worshipped at the tomb of yesterday's thought and drew inspiration from the ideals of earlier ages, which time had made first venerable and then sacred in the eyes of man. It naturally regarded him at first with apprehension, later with alarm, and finally the fear of its members expressed itself in a deadly hate which ended in his martydom. It was repetition of history. The reputation and life of the prophet are always in danger. He will be misrepresented, slandered and misjudged, if he escape the penalty of the death sentence At rare intervals the soul of the prophet and mystic has been found under the robes of a priest, but here usually the priesthood has been arrayed against the iconoclast. Savonarola was a conspicious example of this class.

In the sphere of religion the prophet is ever the advance courier of truth. He blazes the way for the groping multitude. He is impelled onward by the divine afflatus. He is always disquieting. He stimulates reason. He awakes the soul life. He points to the lily and says, Consider. He turns to the sky, glorious in the splendor of dawn or spangled with the silver of night, and exclaims, Behold! He takes up the record of the past, and, in a word, warns against unlimited scepticism and blind credulity. Do not, he urges, reject as wholly worthless, or accept as entirely divine, the accumulated wisdom and follies of ancient days, but search for the truth. He looks into the faces of the thoughtful and says, Come, let us reason together. Consider — behold — search — reason! Thus does the prophet awaken the soul of man. He calls to the sleeping ego to be something more than an animal.

He arouses the divine life, calls into action the higher potentialities of the man's being, and in this way is a saviour to the individual as well as a torch bearer to civilization.

I speak of the prophet and mystic as one; for in truth the distinction is rather of degree than of nature; or, to be more accurate, they are different manifestations of the divine in man. The prophet is an engine in action. He is an aggressive power for righteousness now and here. He mingles with the surging tide of good and evil, a warrior for justice and truth. The mystic ascends the mountains of sprituality and drinks deeply from the divine fountains. The truths of God steal into his soul silently and with an all-pervading influence, as comes the evening dew or the soft light of day. We are told that Jesus, on occasions, doubtless when weary with battling against the powers of evil on every side, and sick at heart for poor, suffering humanity, withdrew into the mountains to pray — that is, to commune with the Infinite.

The mystic craves the inspiration of solitude when torn by the discord of human strife. He posesses a strong intuitional nature. His interior vision is preternaturally developed. He hears, sees, and within his soul *knows* many things which elude the grasp of the self-seeking, business-enthralled struggler upon earth's restless highways. Some time ago I visited a friend who is a scientist and a deep student of the vibratory law. Taking down an instrument somewhat resembling a horn, he handed it to me. I put it to my ear and instantly I heard a great roaring in the room — a noise suggestive of a coming storm. I had merely been able to gather some of the noises present, which without the instrument, had escaped my hearing. Doubtless the reader has often tried the same experiment with a shell. Now, the interior nature of the mystic is so thoroughly awake that his vision penetrates farther than those in whom the spiritual nature is less sensitive, and in moments of exaltation he beholds humanity with face set toward the sky — humanity moving slowly, and often with halting step, but ever moving Godward. He hears the voice of the Infinite, and knows that the ultimate end of all is *Good*. He speaks the words he hears unto those whose eyes are fixed upon the stars.

Sometimes he descends to the seething, struggling world below, where, tiger-like, man devours his fellow-men. Then the mystic not unfrequently becomes the prophet and reformer. In Jesus, we see the perfect blending — the mystic, prophet and reformer; and in our own time we have frequently seen this trinity in unity.

The poet Whittier affords a striking illustration in point. When confronting injustice and inhumanity the sweet-souled Quaker poet became a veritable Isaiah. His anti-slavery verses reveal a soul lost to self and fear, a brain on fire with holy indignation. His words burn into the heart; they fire but do not sear the conscience. They reveal to us a man whose love of justice and freedom has consumed all baser thought. Hear this heart-cry for the honor of the Old Bay State : —

O my God! — for that free spirit, which of old in
    Boston town
Smote the Province House with terror, struck the
    crest of Andros down ! —
For another strong-voiced Adams in the city's
    streets to cry :
"Up for God and Massachusetts ! Set your feet
    on Mammon's lie !
Perish banks and perish traffic, spin your cottons'
    latest pound,
But in Heaven's name keep your honor, — keep the
    heart o' the Bay State sound ! "

So also, in this stanza from "The Crisis," we are reminded of the prophet, who speaks with an authority from within, in bold contrast to the diffident, retiring and mild-mannered Quaker : —

The crisis presses on us; face to face with us it
    stands,
With solemn lips of question, like the Sphinx in
    Egypt's sands !
This day we fashion destiny, our web of fate we
    spin ;
This day for all hereafter choose we holiness or
    sin ;
Even now from starry Gerizim, or Ebal's cloudy
    crown,
We call the dews of blessing or the bolts of cursing
    down!

From the heat and turmoil of the great moral battles which so profoundly aroused the prophet soul, we turn to the poet after he has withdrawn from the forum of public contention — after he has ascended the

mountain, if you will — and hear the calm-
voiced mystic utter thoughts which flood
his soul as the moonlight floods the snow-
crowned mountain peaks : —

Yet sometimes glimpses on my sight,
Through present wrong, the eternal right;
And step by step, since time began,
I see the steady gain of man ;

That all of good the past hath had
Remains to make our own time glad,
Our common, daily life divine,
And every land a Palestine.

Through the harsh noises of our day
A low sweet prelude finds its way ;
Through clouds of doubt and creeds of fear,
A light is breaking, calm and clear.

That song of love, now low and far,
Ere long shall swell from star to star!
That light, the breaking day which tips
The golden-spired apocalypse!

O friend! we need nor rock nor sand,
Nor storied stream of morning-land;

The heavens are glassed in Merrimac —
What more could Jordan render back ?

We lack but open eye and ear
To find the Orient's marvels here —
The still small voice in autumn's hush
Yon maple wood the burning bush.

Henceforth my heart shall sigh no more
For olden time and holier shore ;
God's love and blessing, then and there,
Are now and here and everywhere.

And again he asserts, with that all-sustaining faith which characterizes the true mystic : —

There are, who like the seer of old,
    Can see the helpers God has sent,
And how life's rugged mountain side
    Is white with many an angel tent !

They hear the heralds whom our Lord
    Sends down His pathway to prepare ;
And light, from others hidden, shines
    On their high place of faith and prayer.

Unheard no burdened heart's appeal
　　Moans up to God's inclining ear ;
Unheeded by His tender eye,
　　Falls to the earth no sufferer's tear.

In Gerald Massey, as in Whittier, we find the union of the prophet, reformer and mystic. I am aware that Mr. Massey does not like the term "mystic," holding that he advances nothing which has not been proven to him. Perhaps he would prefer the term "Seer." I use it here in its larger sense of seer — a see-er of things wrapped in mystery and obscurity for the mass of men. This gives the word "Mystic" its truest, noblest sense ; and in this sense I know of no word which so well expresses the meaning I desire to convey.

We have seen with what superb courage he has assailed entrenched wrongs and popular injustice. We have noted his lofty faith, and caught glimpses of the future triumph of right through the mirror of his soul. We now pass to notice the poet as a mystic. In the following lines we have a great thought beautifully expressed :

God hath been gradually forming man
In His own image since the world began,
And is forever working on the soul,
Like sculptor on his statue, till the whole
Expression of the upward life be wrought
Into some semblance of the Eternal thought.
Race after race hath caught its likeness of
The Maker as the eyes grew larger with love.

Here is a companion thought : —

What you call matter is but as the sheath,
Shaped, even as bubbles are, by the spirit-breath.
The mountains are but firmer clouds of earth,
Still changing to the breath that gave them birth.
Spirit aye shapeth matter into view,
As music wears the form it passes through.
Spirit is lord of substance, matter's sole
First cause, formative power, and final goal.

It will be seen that the poet, while discarding the crude ideas and conceptions of creation which were born in the childhood of the human race, opposes the views popular among certain thinkers, who hold that the human brain is merely an expression of physical evolution, and that the law-governed universe, with art, design and intelligence visible in its every phenomenon, is merely the result of force, working blindly and without intelligence. The wonderful facts demonstrated through hypnotism, and the results which have crowned the painstaking and careful research of leading scientists in the fields of psychical phenomena, have by external evidence and incontrovertible facts greatly strengthened the position arrived at by the mystic through the intuitional power and acute interior perception.

Mr. Massey believes that the tree is to be judged by its fruit; that, according as you have performed the will of the Infinite

One, or expressed the best and truest in your life, you shall be rewarded — or, rather, that every good deed bears the doer upward, every real sin lowers the soul. He teaches the high and wholesome morality that, precisely as we help lift and benefit our fellow-men, our souls blossom into the likeness of divinity ; that it is by *deeds of service that the spirit is made royal.* His teaching touching the future of the soul is thus clearly set forth : —

Both heaven and hell are from the human race,
And every soul projects its future place :
Long shadows of ourselves are thrown before,
To wait our coming on the eternal shore.
These either cloth us with eclipse and night,
Or, as we enter them, are lost in light.

There is a striking similarity of thought between the above and these lines of Whittier, although the imagery is entirely different : —

We shape ourselves the joy or fear
    Of which the coming life is made,
And fill our future's atmosphere
    With sunshine or with shade.

The tissue of the life to be
    We weave with colors all our own,
And in the fields of destiny
    We reap as we have sown.

Mr. Massey, while holding that law runs through the universe and that sin brings its own punishment, does not hold to the frightful old-time doctrine that man, environed by sin and surrounded by temptation, having only a few fleeting years in which to obtain wisdom, is nevertheless doomed to be lost for eternity if he falls by the wayside. Such a belief is abhorrent to so broad, tender and noble a nature as his. On this point he says : —

I think heaven will not shut forevermore,
Without a knocker left upon the door,

Lest some belated traveller should come
Heart-broken, asking just to die at home,
So that the Father will at last forgive,
And looking on His face that soul shall live.
I think there will be watchmen through the night,
Lest any, far off, turn them to the light;
That He who loved us into life must be
A Father infinitely fatherly,
And, groping for Him, these shall find their way
From outer dark, through twilight, into day.

I could not sing the song of harvest home,
Thinking of those poor souls that never come;
I could not joy for harvest gathered in,
If any souls, like tares and twitch of sin,
Were flung out by the farmer to the fire,
Whose smoke of torment, rising higher and higher,
Should fill the universe forevermore.

Our science grasps with its transforming hand,
Makes real half the tales of wonderland.
We turn the deathliest fetor to perfume;
We give decay new life and rosy bloom;
Change filthy rags to paper, virgin white,
Make pure in spirit what was foul to sight.
Even dead, recoiling force, to a fairy gift
Of help is turned, and taught to deftly lift.

How can we think God hath no crucible
Save some black country of a burning hell?
Or the great ocean of Almighty power,
No scoop to take the life stream from our shore,
Muddy and dark, and make it pure once more?

Dear God, it seems to me that love must be
The missionary of eternity!
Must still find work, in worlds beyond the grave,
So long as there's a single soul to save;
Gather the jewels that flash Godward in
The dark, down-trodden, toad-like head of sin
That all divergent lines at length will meet,
To make the clasping round of love complete;
The rift 'twixt sense and spirit will be healed,
Before creation's work is crowned and sealed;
The discords cease, and all their strife shall be
Resolved in one vast, peaceful harmony.

Another truth which Mr. Massey frequently expresses is the presence of the Infinite One here and now, in opposition to the narrow view that God spake to His children only in ancient times. Like Whittier, he ever teaches that God is

with us now and here, and that none of
the glory of other days is absent from our
own. In one notable poem he thus
sings : —

There is no gleam of glory gone,
    For those who read in nature's book´;
    No lack of triumph in their look
Who stand in her eternal dawn.

And again, with the calm assurance of
the mystic, he says : —

Not only in old days He bowed
    The heavens and came down ;
We, too, were shadowed by the cloud,
    We saw the glory shown !
The nations that seemed dead have felt
    His coming through them thrill :
Beneath His tread the mountains melt :
    Our God is living still !

He who in secret hears the sigh,
    Interprets every tear,
Hath lightened on us from on high,
    Made known His presence near !

The Word takes flesh, the Spirit form,
  His purpose to fulfil ;
He comes in person of the storm —
  Our God who governs still !

We saw — all of us saw — how He
  Drew sword and struck the blow,
And up and free through their Red Sea
  He bade the captives go :
Yea, we have seen Him, clearly seen
  Him work the miracle :
We know, whate'er may intervene,
  Our God is with us still !

The veil of time a moment falls
  From off the Eternal's face :
Recede the old horizon walls
  To give fresh breathing space :
And all who lift their eyes may learn
  It is our Father's will,
This world to Him shall freely turn,
  A world of freedom still !

The traveller in the valley sees little
of what is around him.   He journeys for a

day up the mountain slope, and his vision is marvellously broadened. Another day's journey toward the peak reveals a still more glorious panorama, and when he reaches the highest crest an almost infinite expanse stretches on every side. So the barbarian caught a contracted and very partial view of God's love and beauty — his own limitation of vision and the animal passions which overmastered him dulled spiritual perception. But as the race rose through countless ages, the conception of the Infinite became expanded, and as the spirit grew more and more sublimated, the real character of the Deity, uncolored by human prejudice and passion, became apparent to the most royal natures. A hint of this thought is given in the last stanza of the above lines.

Few poets have ever thrown into simple words a more beautiful conception of man's relation to God, or God's broad love and

sympathy for his children, who through
past ages have been struggling upward
toward the light, than is found in these
lines of Mr. Massey's : —

This human life is no mere looking-glass,
In which God sees His shadows as you pass.
He did not start the pendulum of time,
To go by law with one great swing sublime,
Resting himself in lonely joy apart :
But to each pulse of life his beating heart.
And, as a parent sensitive, is stirred
By falling sparrow, or heart-wingéd word.

As the babe's life within the mother's dim
And deaf, you dwell in God, a dream of Him.
Ye stir, and put forth feelers which are clasped
By airy hands, and higher life is grasped
As yet but darkly.   Life is in the root,
And looking heavenward, from the ladder-foot,
Wingless as worms, with earthiness fast bound,
Up which ye mount but slowly, round on round,
Long climbing brings ye to the Father's knee ;
Ye open gladsome eyes at last to see
That face of love ye felt so inwardly.

In this vast universe of worlds no waif,
No spirit, looks to Him but floateth safe;
No prayer so lowly but is heard on high;
And if a soul should sigh, and lift an eye,
That soul is kept from sinking with a sigh.

All life, down to the worm beneath the sod,
Hath spiritual relationship to God —
The Life of Life, the love of all, in all;
Lord of the large and infinitely small.

In these verses our poet gives expression to the new religion which is taking possession of the most exalted minds of our day. It is all very well to say that God is so much more than the finest expression of the divine in man that we cannot comprehend Him: but we cannot use this reasonable assumption to bolster up the unreasonable and impossible one that God's attributes are not in alignment with the most perfect ideal which haunts the noblest brains of the best civilization. There are certain eternal verities, the highest and most splendid of which is love. These verities are immutable and unchanging; they form a constellation upon which the eyes of the noblest and most truly divine in all ages have rested. And as humanity in her slow ascent rises to higher altitudes of civilization, a greater number come to appreciate the supreme truth that it is only that which is divine in essence which can yield enduring happiness and spiritual peace. The Golden Rule is not peculiar to any one religion. It has been taught in spirit by philosophers, poets and sages throughout the ages. There are certain fundamental principles in ethics which, by common consent, the highest and purest souls of all lands and periods have regarded as divine; and in proportion as man has given expression to the godlike attributes in his life he has approached earth's highest dream of divinity. The lofty ideal which this dream embodies runs like a thread of gold through every civilization. It was taught by Zoroaster and Confucius, by Gautama and Pythagoras, by the prophets of Israel, and the Stoics of Greece and Rome; it found glorious expression in the life and teaching of Jesus. God, compared with earth's noblest man, may be as the ocean to the rivulet, as the Himalayas to the ant mound; but His nature, if He is the incarnation of what humanity holds as highest, sweetest and truest, must be all that the most divine expression of manhood is, and inconceivably more than this, in *the expression of the divine attributes*. He must be the infinite reservoir of all those virtues which make manhood divine; and being this, He could not do things which would be abhorrent to the noblest man. If at any point throughout the cycle of eternity, He should draw the dead line across which even the weakest of the children He has called into an eternal existence might not fly from darkness and pain into the light, purity and love of a better life, He would be guilty of a crime so abhorrent to an exalted and humane earthly parent that the parent himself would rather die than condemn his offspring to such a fate.

The supreme truth, that God must be better than the best man instead of worse than the most cruel savage, is the keynote of the new evangel which our nineteenth-century prophets and mystics have given the children of men. That is the thought which Whittier, who, in the truest sense, was a mystic, so forcibly put in the following lines : —

> I dare not fix with mete and bound
>   The love and power of God.
>
> *   *   *   *   *
>
> I see the wrong that round me lies,
>   I feel the guilt within ;
> I hear, with groan and travail-cries,
>   The world confess its sin.

Yet, in the maddening maze of things,
    And tossed by storm and flood,
To one fixed trust my spirit clings:
    I know that God is good!

*   *   *   *   *

I know not where His islands lift
    Their fronded palms in air;
I only know I cannot drift
    Beyond His love and care.

This same thought is further impressively taught in the exquiste little allegorical poem, "The Two Angels," in which Whittier gives voice to the conception of God which is the burden of the song of the great poets of our time : —

God called the nearest angels who dwell with Him
    above;
The tenderest one was Pity, the dearest one was
    Love.
"Arise," He said, "my angels! A wail of woe and
    sin
Steals through the gates of heaven, and saddens all
    within.

"My harps take up the mournful strain that from a
    lost world swells,
The smoke of torment clouds the light, and blights
    the asphopels.

"Fly downward to that under world, and on its
    souls of pain
Let Love drop smiles like sunshine, and Pity tears
    like rain!"

Two faces bowed before the throne, veiled in their
    golden hair;
Four white wings lessened swiftly down the dark
    abyss of air.

The way was strange, the flight was long; at last
    the angels came
Where swung the lost and nether world, red-wrap-
    ped in rayless flame.

There Pity, shuddering, wept; but Love, with faith
    too strong for fear,
Took heart from God's almightiness, and smiled a
    smile of cheer.

And lo! that tear of Pity quenched the flame
    whereon it fell,
And, with the sunshine of that smile, hope entered
    into hell!

Two unveiled faces full of joy looked upward to the throne,
Four white wings folded at the feet of Him who sat thereon !

And deeper than the sounds of seas, more soft than falling flake,
Amidst the hush of wing and song the Voice Eternal spake :

"Welcome, my angels! ye have brought a holier joy to heaven ;
Henceforth its sweetest song shall be the song of sin forgiven ? "

In one of his last poems, Tennyson, while the light of the other world was silvering his brow, thus expressed this same conception : —

Doubt no longer that the Highest is the wisest and the best,
Let not all that saddens nature blight thy hope or break thy rest,

  *   *

Neither mourn if human creeds be lower than the
heart's desire!
Through the gates that bar the distance comes a
gleam of what is higher.

Wait till death has flung them open, when the man
will make the Maker
Dark no more with human hatreds in the glare of
deathless fire!

The idea of the Eternal Goodness, in
varying phraseology, has been presented
by almost all the great poets and prophets
of our own time. Gerald Massey, in one
of his terse sentences, says: "*Any God
who demands the worship of fear is unworthy the service of love.*" The new
religion goes out in love to all life. It
binds up the bruises of him who has fallen
by the wayside. It extends the hand to
the sinking. It calls aloud for justice for
the weak and oppressed. It denounces
tyranny, injustice and whatsoever lowers
manhood or degrades womanhood. It de-

mands that the rights of the child and those of the mother be sacredly and inviolably kept. It whispers hope and love to the despairing. It gives voice to the words which come from above in the most exalted songs of our time. It teaches the kinship of man to God in such a way that the old-time nightmare disappears. And as the child, with open arms and joyous cry, rushes to meet the loved parent, so do earth's children go to the Father above for that sustaining power and holy peace which through all past time sages have drawn from the Infinite. This thought is beautifully set forth by Mr. Massey in the following lines : —

There is no pathway Man hath ever trod,
By faith or seeking sight, but ends in God.
Yet 'tis in vain ye look Without to find
The inner secrets of the Eternal mind,
Or meet the King on His external throne.
But when ye kneel at heart, and feel so lone,

Perchance behind the veil you get the grip
And spirit-sign of secret fellowship ;
Silently as the gathering of a tear
The human want will bring the Helper near:
The very weakness that is utterest need
Of God, will draw Him down with strength indeed.

In the province of religious thought, Mr. Massey has been a herald of the new day. His utterances are deeply spiritual, yet charmingly rational. While recognizing the interior self as the true ego, and fully appreciating the spiritual forces underlying creation, he abhors superstition, and is filled with a holy passion for a more complete knowledge of life. He cannot understand why men should place prejudice above truth, and believes it to be the sacred duty of every man, woman and child, to use the divine torch of reason to guide his steps. He is a thorough believer in evolution, and hails modern science as the handmaid of progress. In a word, Gerald Massey is a child of the dawn.

Civilization's Inferno; or, Studies in the Social Cellar. By B. O. Flower.

A bold, unconventional work, which in a merciless manner lays bare the criminal extravagance, the disgusting flunkyism, and the immorality found in what the author terms the "Froth of Society."

It fearlessly contrasts the criminal extravagance and moral effeminacy of the slothful rich with the terrible social, moral and physical condition of the ignorant, starving, and degraded poor.

It carries the reader into the social cellar where uninvited poverty abounds, and from there into the sub-cellar, or the world of the criminal poor.

It is rich in suggestive hints, and should be in the hands of every thoughtful man and woman in America.

Absorbingly interesting and at times thrilling, no one can read its pages without being made better for the perusal.

Handsomely Bound in Cloth; Price, $1.00.

The Arena Publishing Company, - Boston, Mass.

Press Criticisms of Civilization's Inferno.

It is a truthful and graphic delineation of the condition of the people in the social undertow. Mr. Flower has a keen and profound sympathy with the difficulties that the poor are laboring under, and he describes what he has seen with his own eyes in terms that chill one's blood. He does not hesitate to call things by their right names, and points out the magnitude of the peril, showing that no palliative measures will satisfy people.—*Daily Herald, Boston.*

It is a strong appeal to the Christian civilization of the times to arise and change the current of human misery which in these modern times is driving with such resistless force.—*Chicago Daily Inter-Ocean.*

A book which should be read and studied by all. Mr. Flower's high enthusiasm, the artistic impulse which has guided his pen, together with his intimate knowledge gained by personal investigation of the matter, make his book most admirable.—*Boston Times.*

It is not only the record made of discoveries during a period of systematic slumming, but it is also a philosophical view of the dangers of the conditions which he discusses.—*Chicago Times.*

The work is a masterly presentation of social conditions around us. These make a vast problem, and it is by such earnest thinkers as Mr. Flower that they will be solved.—*Chicago Herald.*

A thoughtful work by a thoughtful man, and should turn the minds of many who are now ignorant or careless to the condition of the countless thousands who live in the "social cellar." No one can read the book without feeling that the author's diagnosis of the case is true and gives each one his own personal responsibility.—*Courier Journal, Louisville, Ky.*

This work has created a decided sensation throughout the country, and has raised considerable controversy between the author and other writers on the one hand, and society's leaders on the other. It is a fresh presentation from personal observation of the facts of poverty, destitution, squalor, and oppression that exists in every large city in the world.—*Burlington Hawkeye, Burlington, Iowa.*

Society, as it is now constituted, is nothing less than a sleeping volcano. Who dares to say how soon the upheaval will come, or whether it can be evaded by the adoption of prompt measures of relief? Certainly the condition of the lower social strata calls for immediate action on the part of those whose safety is at stake. Mr. Flower has accomplished a great work, in setting forth the exact truth of the matter, without any effort at palliation. It will be well indeed for the prosperous classes of the community if they are warned in time.—*Boston Beacon.*

What general Booth has done for London and Mr. Jacobs Riis for New York, Mr. Flower has done for cultured Boston. He is a professional man of letters, and tells his story with the skill and knack of his craft.—*Daily Constitution, Atlanta, Ga.*

A powerfully written book, presenting facts which ought to move the most sluggish soul to resolve and action. Its whole lesson, sad as it is, is one that needs to be learned; and we will not detract from its completeness by presenting it in fragments; but we desire to call special attention to the author's exposition of the facts, concerning which there has been so much scepticism, that the rich are growing richer and the poor poorer. If there is any lingering belief or hope in the mind of anybody that his statement is a mere partisan bugaboo, as it has sometimes been styled, Mr. Flower's book will settle the matter.—*Daily Free Press, Detroit, Mich.*

He literally uncaps the pit, the hell on earth; and if there are "the pleasures of sin for a season," it will be seen that the season is not a long one. The author depicts the scenes he has witnessed, and has the moral purpose—the passion for a better estate—which, enlivening his pages, makes the book as wholesome as it is inciting to practical endeavor.—*Christian Leader, Boston.*

In this book the great social problem of the day is laid before the reader in all its importance, its increasing dangers are pointed out, and practical remedies suggested in a way that is as interesting as thoughtful. We are glad to see the fashionable extravagances and vices of the class that assumes for itself the title of " society " treated with the condemnation they deserve. It is a work that has long been needed, and we are sure it will go far toward the end it looks forward to so hopefully.—*Nassua Literary Magazine, published by senior class of Princeton University.*

A volume of remarkable interest and power, and merits the careful attention of all students of social problems.—*Boston Daily Traveller.*

The New Time : A Plea for the Union of the Moral Forces for Practical Progress.

This new work, by the author of " Civilization's Inferno," deals with practical methods for the reform of specific social evils, which are capable of vast diminution and of ultimate abolition. The writer does not bind together a mere bundle of social speculations, that would seem to many to have only a remote and abstract relevance to everyday life. He deals with facts within every one's knowledge.

The Table of Contents, briefly sketched, gives perhaps the very best idea of its practical aims, both immediate and ulti_mate : —

I. UNION FOR PRACTICAL PROGRESS.—The widespread desire for the union of all who wish to help the world onward. — Is it practical? — Some things which have been accomplished.

II. THEY HAVE FALLEN INTO THE WINEPRESS.—Olive Schreiner's " Visions of Hell," and its application to present conditions — The out-of-work, homeless ones in our midst — Moral obliquity in the young — Education, justice and freedom the remedies — Some suggestive hints.

III. JESUS OR CÆSAR.—The opportunity of the Church — The rise of the spirit of Cæsar — The spirit and teachings of Jesus — The hope of the republic — How each one may hasten a brighter day.

IV. THE NEW TIME.— The heart-hunger of our time — The work before us — The elevation and emancipation of humanity through education and justice — Crying evils and great reforms which demand the attention of thoughtful people — The duty and responsibility of the individual — Some helpful illustrations — The starving and shelterless Chriss at our door — Fundamental and palliative remedies — Let the next step be evolutionary.

V. THEN DAWNED A LIGHT IN THE EAST. — A Suggestive lesson from the history of the civilization of two thousand years ago — Society in Rome under the Cæsars — The hectic flush of death — Intellectual training without moral culture — An age of artificiality — Civilization in Palestine — The rise of a great, serene soul in the midst of a society permeated by cant and hypocrisy — The three great redemptive words, Faith, Hope and Love; their influence two thousand years ago — Present conditions — Our duty — The present no time for idleness or pessimism — The dawn is purpling the east.

Handsome Cloth : Price, $1.00.

Press Criticisms of New Time.

It is a fervent plea for the union and practical co-operation of all those who are interested in the welfare of humanity, and who believe that it is their duty to do their utmost toward alleviating the sufferings of their less fortunate fellow mortals. Mr. Flower is a firm believer in the ultimate triumph of the spirit of fraternity and justice, and in this little book he suggests how this spirit may be fostered throughout the United States. There are many loving souls, he claims, in every city, town and village, who would fain spend most of their lives in aiding their fellows, and he maintains that a wondrous amount of good would be the result if only these scattered children of light could be properly organized. Undoubtedly he is right, and it would not surprise us if this idea took root. We may not all possess Mr. Flower's enthusiasm, but we must all admire the eloquence with which he pictures the " new time " for which he yearns, the time when all men will be brothers and justice will rule the earth.—*New York Herald.*

Mr. Flower takes his stand on the side of human progress. In the book "The New Time," he enters a vigorous, earnest and touching plea for the union of warring sects in the great cause of the amelioration of human misery, whether it arises from poverty or guilt.

Without being in any respect a sermon, Mr. Flower's work has all the force and convincing power of the pulpit. Indeed it has more, for the pulpit is often enough the vehicle of the denunciation of opposing sects — a fact which occasionally mars its usefulness in the eyes of every reflecting man. Mr. Flower's book touches briefly on the causes of much of human suffering and crime, and proceeds to show how a real and permanent union of Christian workers of all denominations can be achieved and what noble results will spring from such a union.

Such a union as he points out has long been the dream of the humanitarian, but up to the present the jealousy of sect has prevented it from being realized. For many years, however, the Christian world has been gradually brought closer together, and the work of consolidation is still going on. The time will probably never come when all religions will be merged in each other, nor is it necessary for the cause of Christian union, as Mr. Flower understands it, that it should. All he pleads for is that the churches should join together in the common cause of elevating the poor and the wretched, nor is it necessary that in so doing they should sacrifice any essential part of their doctrines.

The Parliament of Religions gave a stronger impetus to the movement for Christian union than anything that has been done or anything that has been written for a couple of centuries past, and that noble conference is bearing and has borne noble fruit. Much, nevertheless, remains to be done.

Hundreds of thousands must be reached by individual persuasion. Much of the literature that is to do this yet remains to be written, but if the writers of it shall model themselves on the liberality, tolerance and true Christianity which characterizes Mr. Flower's work, the end in view may not be so very far off after all.—*Daily Item*, Philadelphia, Pa.

The inspiration of a new social order seems to have suddenly assumed the proportions of a contagion. Prophets are springing up all over the land, and new books from every quarter of the globe. The real import of God's love for the world seems to be dawning upon the mind of thinkers for the first time in social history, and reformers are just beginning to catch the inspiration of the Christ-life. These books are by no means accordant as yet, but they are sufficiently harmonious in design to impress the student with the fact that the kingdom of heaven is about to begin on earth. Almost all modern writers on social conditions are so imbued with the altruistic spirit that altruism seems to be the " Elias " of the new era.

So prominent indeed is this spirit in the above work that one almost feels that its author is the John the Baptist of the time about which he prophesies, and that he should at once demand baptism at his hands — that is, a baptism of his spirit. We cannot have too many such books as this at this time. It was not written for the sake of the book nor its author, but of humanity. It is a plain yet earnest and vigorous presentation of some of our social conditions, with suggestions, not a few of which are entirely practical and full of promise. It has little of the visionary and speculative in it and proposes immediate action upon practical grounds for the purpose of the earliest possible relief and solution of our troubles —*Christian Evangelist*, St. Louis, Mo.

Like whatever Mr. Flower writes, the book has to do with a *practical*, immediate means of helping humanity in the throes of its upward struggle. Humanity as a mass of course contains the leavening lump of spirituality which will ultimately express itself as a matter of course in the very reforms we so much desire. Equally of course do the consciously-spiritual workers assist in this process—this forms one of the pleasures as well as duties of the enlightened state.

And it is just such an influence as this Union for Practical Progress that sets emotions and movements working which need almost but a touch to overspread the sky with a blaze of glory—the glory of awakened humanity. It is incalculable, the good to be accomplished by concerted plans, organized in individual places but all with one central purpose and animated by one central desire. The name of the organization is a good one too, appealing to everyone, everywhere. *Practical* progress is what we need, and aid toward that end *cannot* fail of eager appreciation. The movement by its nature appeals to the higher faculties, arouses and puts them in working order — and by this means *anything* may be accomplished.

In such a cause we know of no one who does more valiant work than Mr. Flower. Convinced of its "righteousness," he will pursue it to its ultimate personally, and arouse in hosts of others both desire and determination to do likewise. Such work is of inestimable value — and in this connection everyone should realize that every person is helping his fellow if he but live on the highest plane of which he is conscious, also striving constantly to get still higher by helping to raise others —*Boston Ideas*, Boston, Mass.

Lessons Learned from Other Lives.

A BOOK OF SHORT BIOGRAPHIES, WRITTEN FOR YOUNG PEOPLE.

CONTENTS.—I. THE PHILOSOPHER, Seneca and Epictetus. II. THE WARRIOR MAID, Joan of Arc. III. THE STATESMAN, Henry Clay. IV. THE ACTOR, Edwin Booth, Joseph Jefferson. V. THE POET, John Howard Payne, William Cullen Bryant, Edgar Allan Poe, Alice Cary, Phœbe Cary, J. G. Whittier, VI. THE SCIENTIST, Alfred Russel Wallace. VII. THE MANY-SIDED GENIUS, Victor Hugo.

PRESS COMMENTS.

A highly interesting and instructive work —*Daily Telegraph, Hartford, Conn.*

A readable and helpful book. Mr. Flower is an earnest, thoughtful, radical, compact writer. Many who gladly read these sketches will be made nobler and braver thereby.—*Education, Boston, Mass.*

This is a delightful book to read. It is written with exquisite taste and tenderness. It effloresces with a literary aroma. The author has sought a fair and favored field in which to find mental rumination. His effort is an idyl of life's faire t forms and figures He is a young, brilliant writer. The book sparkles with lite ary jewels —*Christian Leader, Cincinnati, O.*

An admirable collection of brief biographical sketches, each teaching by some anecdote or illustration the prominent characteristic of the life under consideration Among those selected we note Joan of Arc, Henry Clay, Joe Jefferson, Bryant, Poe, Whittier, A. R. Wallace, and Victor Hugo The sketches are brightly written and the salient points in each life well brought out. Many of the best poems of the poets named are given.—*The States, New Orleans, La.*

B. O. Flower, editor of THE ARENA, has given to biographical literature one of the most charming books it has ever been our good fortune to read. The book in question is entitled " Lessons Learned from Other Lives." It is written in a delightfully easy style, and many of the lives are of personal friends of the author.—*Every Saturday, Elgin, Ill.*

The Arena Publishing Company, of Boston, has recently issued an attractive volume entitled " Lessons Learned from Other Lives " Mr. B. O. Flower, the well-known editor of THE ARENA, has given us under this name a number of brief historiettes illustrative of different phases of character. Mr Flower modestly dedicates his work more especially to the young; but the admirable style, the terseness, and keen analysis of the e ch racter sketches will recommend them to all classes of readers. Biography should be especially interesting but not every one has the ability to render it so Mr Flower has this happy faculty to an unusual extent. His essays are equal to his editorials, and more cannot be said.—*Rocky Mountain Daily News, Denver, Col.*

Lightning Source UK Ltd.
Milton Keynes UK
UKHW012200301118
333276UK00011B/1581/P